Wise, Happy and Feeling Good

Wise, Happy and Feeling Good
Maxims on Life, Success and Well-Being

Jarl Forsman & Steve Sekhon

GRATITUDE 24/7
EVOLVE YOUR THINKING

High Vibration Publishing
Sausalito, California

High Vibration Publishing
Sausalito, CA

© 2013 Jarl Forsman & Steve Sekhon

All rights reserved. Published 2013.

No part of this book may be used or reproduced in any manner without written permission of the author and publisher.

ISBN 978-0-9849587-1-9

Please direct inquiries and correspondence to:

info@gratitudetwentyfourseven.com

Acknowledgment

Many thanks to Chuck Scurich for his talented and meticulous copyediting.

A big thanks to Kyle Hoobin for his skillful help in designing the cover.

"Jarl and Steve have created a beautiful collection of powerful words of wisdom. Concise, elegant, heartfelt and each one packed with valuable knowledge. This book is sure to help anyone looking to experience more of life's daily grace and fulfillment."

Howard Falco, author of
I AM: The Power of Discovering Who You Really Are

"*Wise, Happy and Feeling Good* is filled with nourishing gems that will open your heart. With delightful brevity Jarl and Steve have written insightful reminders that encourage you to live more in the moment, find your authentic self and allow greater fulfillment."

Gerald Jampolsky, M.D., author of *Love is Letting Go of Fear* and *A Mini Course for Life*, with Diane Cirincione, Ph.D.

Introduction

Above the clouds, fog and rain, there's a limitless expanse of crystal clear, blue sky. Beneath the layers of thoughts, worries and fears, there's a place in your mind that's still, calm and quiet. Just as you can fly above the clouds and find blue sky, you can focus and relax your mind to find stillness and peace beneath the chatter.

You alone determine your experience of life by choosing where to focus your attention. When you look for problems, you find them. When you look for solutions, you find *them*. When you run with the chatter in your mind, you experience confusion and weariness. When you look for peace, you find stillness and joy.

The peaceful ground of being inside each person can only be found in the present moment, when the mind is free of thoughts of the past or future. The more time you spend cultivating this present moment peacefulness, the more joyful, relaxed and trusting you become.

We started Gratitude Twenty Four Seven to share the understanding that we developed through years of inquiry and daily practice. The practice that's made the most substantial improvement in the quality of our lives has two parts.

The first is to intentionally cultivate only thoughts and words that are in alignment with what we *want* to create rather than unconsciously focus on what we *don't* want. This is of the utmost importance because thoughts have creative power. You energize whatever you spend time thinking about.

The second part is to focus on gratitude as often as possible. This practice will raise your energetic vibration and help you develop a natural harmony with people and circumstances that have the kind of high quality energy you want to be around and embody yourself.

The secret to positive transformation lies in understanding the connection between the thoughts you cultivate and the feelings that result from those thoughts. The key to developing this understanding is becoming *conscious* of the way you interpret and consequently experience life.

You truly are the creator of your life experience. It's up to you to be conscious of what you create. This is one of the most powerful approaches to finding lasting fulfillment, peace and joy in life. It's the secret to feeling good.

Imagine a planet populated with fulfilled and joyful people! Will you join us by growing your own happiness quotient and sharing it with the world? Together, we can evolve the consciousness of the planet.

This book is comprised of the highlights from one year of published maxims from our website Gratitude Twenty Four Seven. It is our hope that you benefit as much from reading these pages as we have from writing them.

With love and light,

Jarl Forsman and Steve Sekhon

Love Your Life

Every time you appreciate something, you're being nice to yourself. You don't need scientific evidence to prove the positive effects of loving thoughts. Just take a look at someone in love.

Then *be* one!

The Benefits of Brevity

The best jokes and stories often use the fewest words to get to the point. The same technique works for your troubles too. When you don't complain or add extra verbiage, you make it possible for them to turn into good stories. Or at the very least, fade away more quickly.

Less is more.

You Get to Choose

What you focus on creates your experience of life. You're free to choose where to put your attention in every moment. Do you focus on light or dark, right or wrong, thorns or roses?

Stopped to smell any lately?

How to Improve Any Relationship

Think of someone who irritates you and commit to thinking only positive thoughts about them. Do it every time you think of them and notice how your attitude changes. Your inner dialogue is what makes you feel the way you do.

Changing *that* changes everything.

Eyes on the Prize

No matter what shows up in your reality, keep your mind on what you want. Have patience and don't be attached to things turning out exactly as you envision. Expect success and be grateful in anticipation. Visualize yourself beaming at the results.

Enjoy the power of positive focus.

Harmony Lies Beneath

Harmony is the natural state of the Universe. It's only your perception and interpretation of reality that convinces you otherwise. If you're out of harmony with a person or situation 'out there,' ask your Inner Sage to show you how everything is perfect.

It is, beneath your thoughts.

Choose Wisely

If you see yourself as a victim, life will generously provide you with hardships. If you see yourself as a student of life, it will present you with perfect lessons. When you become a master, you'll see the perfection in the lessons *and* the hardships. The transition from student to master requires conscious daily effort; from victim to student, just a choice.

A very good one.

Choosing Possibilities

In the face of difficulty, you can worry about undesired outcomes or look for opportunity. The possibilities are endless when you step out of your box and open to new ways of thinking. Think of something you find challenging and ask your Inner Presence to energize your creative thinking about it.

Limitless potential.

A Simple Shift of Attention

Whether you're agitated, anxious or angry, you still have complete freedom to choose where to place your focus. When you divert your attention from problems toward solutions, you feel good. Just as you would divert a child's attention away from something that isn't good for them, you can do the same for yourself. It's the vibration of your thinking that determines the quality of your life.

Raise them both.

Getting the Most Out of Life

Getting the most out of what you do requires paying attention. The more tuned in you are to the present moment, the more you notice. The more you notice, the deeper your experience. The deeper the experience, the richer it feels. The richer it feels, the richer you are.

Attention pays off.

Gratitude Begets Gratitude

A marvelous consequence of feeling grateful is that it creates a propensity inside you to keep feeling that way. It's a powerful gift you can give to yourself...

That keeps on giving.

Giving Enriches

Your life is not measured by what you have but by what you give. Whether it's a smile, a hand or an endowment, you make a difference with each offering. When your focus is self-centered, you never seem to have enough. When you share with others, you experience abundance.

Get enriched quick.

Snowball Effect

Thinking thoughts of gratitude and appreciation throughout the day spirals you emotionally upward. The more you focus on what you like, the more you see things to like. It's a snowball effect in the best possible way.

Roll with it!

Make It Feel Good

The great news is that you are 100 % responsible for how you feel. Before you put your spin on it, nothing means anything. No matter what anyone says to you, it's only your interpretation that creates your feelings. Even when you are positively sure someone intends to slight you, you have the option to resist slighting yourself by remembering, "this is theirs, not mine".

You've got the power!

Tell It Like You Want It

The past is merely fragmented memories woven into a story that changes according to how you tell it. You can alter the impact your past has on you by changing your story about it. Gratitude and forgiveness make all the difference.

Weave it with love.

An Energy Boost

To sweeten your emotional life, take a look at your thought patterns. Inner complaining dampens your emotional environment and drains your energy. If you catch yourself complaining, shift your attention to what you do like. Since what you focus on expands, quickly replace the complaint with a thought of gratitude and feel your energy level increase. Big changes come by taking small steps.

You'll be waltzing in no time.

Be Grateful Now

You won't be happy with what you get until you're happy with what you've got. Habits develop a momentum. Get in the habit of going with the good.

Gratitude pays off.

You Get What You Give

The best way to get what you want is to give it freely. The outside world is a mirror reflecting back who and what you are. Everyone seems friendly when you are. No one is more lovable than someone who loves. If you feel you lack something, give it to yourself and others. Then notice how everyone starts giving it to you.

Like a smile.

Train Your Mind

Rolling through life with a healthy, happy mindset is a matter of practice. Scientific studies show that how you feel is not the result of where you are, what you do or what you have, but rather how you think. It takes conscious effort to train your mind to stay focused on positive outcomes. Once you get the hang of it, you'll never forget how to do it.

Just like riding a bike.

Survey, Accept, Design and Build

Whether building a cabin or a castle, your masterpiece will be influenced by the lay of the land. Only after surveying and accepting the existing conditions, can you effectively create your dream. The same goes for life. You have to accept each situation, as it is, before you can effectively determine what you'll do to alter or improve it. Survey, accept, design, and build.

It works for just about everything.

We're Making It All Up!

Shakespeare said, "There is nothing either good or bad, but thinking makes it so." When you understand this, your life improves radically. Your version of the world is based on how you perceive and judge 'what is.' Focusing on things that make you grateful enhances your experience.

Live life in high-definition.

Try a Little Love

If you are out of harmony with a family member, friend, co-worker or even a politician, imagine sending them compassion and love. Visualize a beam that emanates from you and shines on them like a spotlight. Radiating love and compassion nurtures and transforms you *and* your target. You won't have to imagine the results...

You'll experience them.

You're the Boss

Admitting that you're in control of your emotional destiny can be daunting. But only until you feel the tremendous relief that comes from knowing that you choose the quality of every experience. When you fully own this power, you can never be a victim.

You're in charge.

Being Is the Goal

Life won't be really satisfying until you get in touch with your authentic self. How do you do that? Don't believe the negative thoughts that you think about yourself. They're almost all constructed from bits and pieces of feedback you've heard from others. The real you is joyfully experiencing life moment by moment. No past and no future.

Just now.

The Big A

You can go to great lengths to get attention from the outside, but the only way to really get enough of it is to give it to yourself. Until you do, you won't believe it, even if the whole world is applauding. Give yourself a hand first.

Then everyone else will too.

Just for Fun

What if life is just for fun? Imagine getting to the end of your life and finding out that the whole purpose was just to enjoy it. Would you change anything now?

Play time.

Look for What's Working

It's energizing to focus on what's going well in your life. Make a list of ten things you like about yourself and notice how good it feels. With the energy boost you get from focusing on what's right, even the things that aren't tend to right themselves naturally.

Like a buoy.

Night at the Oscars

You're the writer, producer, director and actor of the movie called *Your Life*. If you could just snap your fingers to make it happen, how would you change the script? Since you're already playing all these roles, why not play them with intention?

Now, write your acceptance speech.

Love Boomerang

Your mind has no boundaries. When you think loving thoughts about someone else, they feel it, whether they're aware of it or not. That phone call from the very person you were thinking of was not a coincidence. The quality of your thoughts are felt and radiated back to you in kind.

Ricochet.

Outside the Box

New inventions originate from minds that dare to venture beyond convention. If you have a dream that seems wild and crazy, remember people used to think the Earth was flat.

Go for it.

Labor of Love

The reward for work is in the doing. Working for the joy of it requires no outside approval, increases the quality of your output and enhances your mood.

Work like it's play.

Circle or Spiral

Everything moves in cycles. If you stick to the same old routine and avoid challenges, you end up going in circles. If you step outside your comfort zone and expand your horizons, you spiral up...

The evolutionary ladder.

Right or Kind?

Next time you disagree with someone, ask yourself if you'd rather be right or kind. In the game of right and wrong, someone has to be wrong. In the game of kind everyone wins.

Seems kind of right.

You're the Gardener

Are you planting peace and joy? Every thought you cultivate is a seed sown in the garden of your life. Plant the seeds you want to see bloom. If you pluck the weeds quickly enough, they won't have time to sprout. It's the best gardening you can do for the planet.

Thought weeding.

To Love or Be Loved

Is it more satisfying in the hearts of noble beings to love or to be loved? *That* is the question. The answer? To love! When you give love, you feel it. Whereas you could easily be loved and not even know it. It's nice to see that beam in someone's eyes when they look at you, but it's even sweeter when it's radiating out from you.

Beam forth.

Lemonade Stand

The tree of life drops a lemon every now and then. Your experience doesn't depend nearly so much on what actually happens to you, as it does on how you handle it. The most loving thing you can do for yourself is make lemonade.

Then share it.

B Natural

When you are loose, natural and relaxed, life flows. You think more clearly, your body is happier and you're more fun to be around. You are neither too sharp, nor too flat.

Pitch perfect.

Master This

Peace of mind comes from understanding that yesterday's thoughts and actions created your experience of today, just as today's thoughts and actions will create your experience of tomorrow. By choosing your thoughts wisely, you develop self-mastery.

The kind that matters.

The Right Frequency

Every thought radiates a frequency that defines your experience. When you become consciously aware of the quality of your thoughts, you begin to choose ones that make life more satisfying.

Start with gratitude.

Correct and Continue

Everyone makes mistakes. Mentally reliving them over and over while wishing they never happened just keeps them alive. Turn mistakes into learning tools and grow from them. Take note, visualize how you'll act differently if you have the chance and then let go.

Lessons in disguise.

Thoughts Create

If you trust that things will work out well, they will. If you think solutions aren't easy to find, they won't be. Every thought and word helps shape your future. Be sure you're thinking and speaking in alignment with what you want to create.

Joyful thinking makes a joyful life.

Desires Seek Fulfillment

No matter what you desire, imagine you have it, feel it and then let go of attachment to it showing up in exactly the form you imagine. Be open to accepting the feeling of fulfillment however it appears. After all, it's what you're really after.

Serial fulfillment.

Little Tests

If you have a negative reaction to something, feel it and then consciously turn your thoughts to harmony and love. Pretend it's just a test to measure your commitment to living in peace. Make sure to keep healthy boundaries in place and radiate love to everyone. Above all, avoid unpleasant thought repetition.

Ace the test.

The Real You

When you're talking to yourself, have you ever wondered which voice is the real you: the one talking or the one listening? Pay attention, the real you is compassionate and inclusive. The false one compares, criticizes and complains. Listen to the real one.

It's the voice of love.

Be Considerate

It's not what you do that matters, but how you do it. It's not what you say, but how you say it. Almost anything can be said or done kindly with the right intention and thoughtfulness. Take time to be considerate, it's worth the effort.

Consider it.

Your Biggest Fan

Admiration from others doesn't necessarily result in happiness. In fact, having your contentment depend upon praise from others is a risky proposition. It's better to be clear about your values and live in alignment with your own code.

Admire yourself.

Desires Are Gifts

Desires are gifts arising to give you direction. If your attempt to satisfy a desire isn't beneficial to all involved, it won't end up feeling good to you either. Wait until you see how everyone can win...then take action.

Better results.

Glorious Riches

Good health is no big deal…until you're sick. A harmonious relationship feels routine…until a disagreement erupts. Simple and wonderful riches abound every day. Take the time to acknowledge the ones you may be taking for granted.

Be thankful.

True Wealth

You have true wealth when you're grateful for what you have right now, no matter how meager. Without appreciation, you can have it all and still want more. Gratitude creates a river of fulfillment that flows directly to your door.

Let it in.

Love Radiation

When people you love are suffering, the best thing you can do is radiate love and compassion to them. Suffering along with them just adds more suffering. Modeling peace and harmony is the most helpful thing you can possibly do for everyone.

Be a light.

Exit Reaction

It's rare to settle differences in the heat of a disagreement. Understanding is difficult to achieve with the same mindset that created the discord. Take some time out and resume the conversation after you're both ready to find peace and harmony. Once you've sincerely listened to each other, you can even find peace in agreeing to disagree.

Opinions vary.

Reach

Some days you have to reach a little more deeply to find joy. Take the time to look for what's right and feel the mojo of gratitude. It turns ordinary days into remarkable ones.

Personal training.

The Big Picture

Being overly concerned with setbacks and delays can cause stress. When you fly at 30,000 feet, you understand that little bumps and dips are part of the journey. A switchback mountain road still gets you to the top, often with richer experiences, deeper understanding and greater rewards.

Zoom out and lighten up.

Own It

The only thing absolutely consistent with everything you experience is that you are there when it happens. Taking responsibility for your part is the key to moving on. Until you understand this truth, you'll continue to receive opportunities to help you learn it.

What you resist persists.

Like a Planet

You have a magnetic force that pulls experiences, opportunities and people to you. Your habitual thoughts create the quality of this force. If you want to see better things in your orbit, change the quality of your thoughts. Gratitude does the trick.

Cultivate appreciation.

Savor the Moment

Nothing in life is permanent. The best strategy to achieve happiness is to savor every moment, welcome each experience as a blessing and treat one another with the kindness you would like to receive yourself.

It's an amazing present.

The Charm of Humility

Who would you rather be around: the brainy, articulate person who's always trying to prove themselves right, or the person who listens thoughtfully, considers different points of view and acknowledges that there might be more than one right answer?

No brainer.

Learn to Discern

To reach your goals, you have to be able discern what you do and don't like. This is different from criticizing and complaining. Keep your attention on what you prefer and watch it grow.

Discern and learn.

Imagine the Solution

What you give your attention to moment by moment will determine your experience of life. If you want more joy, keep your mind on what you love. You can't experience peace by paying attention to something painful, even if you're trying to change it. Instead, imagine it's already solved and let the 'how' reveal itself to you.

Effortless success.

Why Compare

You are one of a kind. Comparing yourself to others is like comparing apples to oranges. Listen to your heart - it's your guidance system. It's the only way to live an authentic and deeply satisfying life. You're an instrument.

Play your own tune.

The Fallacy of Pressure

Pressure is a clumsy way to motivate your self. It's so much more pleasant to decide what you want, apply the appropriate effort and watch things unfold with grace. No need to inflict unnecessary worry and stress - it doesn't improve the outcome.

Suffering is optional.

Think Solution

Challenges and difficulties are easier to overcome with the right attitude. Circumstances don't determine how you feel, your thoughts do. Redirect your thoughts to what you're looking for...

Solutions.

The Peaceful Present

If you want peace of mind, notice how good things are in this very moment. The present generally contains all that you need. Don't borrow problems from the future. When the future comes, solutions will come with it.

Don't feed the hypothetical monster.

Self-Love Fulfills

When you truly love yourself and have a deep appreciation for your life, you don't need to look to the outside world for satisfaction. The world mirrors your degree of fulfillment. If there's anything you want and don't have, look to see where you lack appreciation.

Then find it.

Fresh Air

The place for drama is on the stage or the big screen. The more mature you are, the less tolerance you have for blame, shame and guilt. Finding fault creates more stress. When you accept what's showing up now and look for how it's right, you're like a breath of fresh air.

Refreshing.

Internal Consistency

When you behave in alignment with your values, you act with integrity. When you diverge from what you feel is right, you go out of balance. Be honest about whether or not you live up to your own code and take action to get into alignment as needed.

You'll love yourself for doing it.

Nobody's Infallible

Nobody gets it right all of the time. Understanding this makes you more compassionate toward other people and their mistakes. Sometimes, admitting that you're wrong opens doors, softens stances and enhances credibility.

Right is relative.

Your Body Is Your Vehicle

Every car needs a tune-up. Every body needs one too. The best mechanic for that job is your mind. Gratitude is the tool.

Use it.

Daily Practice

Daily practice creates mastery - whether of a valued skill or an unwanted habit. Take a look at what you are mastering intentionally or otherwise. Drop the practices that don't serve you.

Master appreciation.

Pregnant with Possibility

Every single moment is filled with unlimited potential. Fear and worry about the future can obscure that potential from view. Free yourself from limiting beliefs. Dare to approach every moment like it's the first you've ever experienced. This moment has within it all you need.

Beginner's mind.

Is It Real?

Two people can encounter the same situation, have totally different experiences and both believe that their own version is accurate. That's because outer circumstances don't create your experience, your beliefs do. You're free to change those if you want.

Free will.

Grow Your Love Garden

If you want more love in your life, love your life more. Love is not something that someone gives you, but rather something you generate yourself. You only feel love when you give love. Practice loving something about everything and everyone you encounter.

Cultivate it!

Faith or Fear

Both faith and fear result from beliefs. Faith is the belief that things will turn out well. Fear is the belief that they won't. As long as you're engaging in the 'what if' game, you might as well make it feel good. Which one serves you?

Choose wisely.

Eliminate Your Big 'But'

How many times have you been in the perfect situation, where everything was just right except one, little thing? Learn to identify and drop the habit of focusing on the one thing that isn't quite right. Enjoy the 99% that's perfect.

Reduce your but.

Thought Patrol

Your thoughts determine the quality of your life. Each thought has a vibratory frequency which not only affects your mood, but also the world around you. Cultivate the thoughts you'd like to manifest.

Skip the rest.

Vantage Point

Time brings perspective. In the middle of a crisis, nothing is as compelling as the issue at hand. One month later, it's less of a big deal. One year later, you see how it was perfect. After a couple of years, it's one of your best stories.

The big picture.

The Answer Is NOW

Stressful thoughts are usually about the future. Don't miss the bounty of the present moment by worrying about things to come. If you're looking too far ahead, you might miss valuable solutions available in this very moment.

Tune in to K-NOW.

Accept Thyself

Strategies to gain approval from others are futile. Until you give it to yourself, no amount of adulation will suffice. Look within for acceptance and love. When you love yourself, everything else follows.

You lead.

The Right Spirit

The only reason you ever want anything is because you think it will make you happier. By the time you get it, your mind has already come up with something else to want. This is natural and healthy if done in the right spirit. If not, it will keep you chasing fulfillment forever. The trick is to find your happiness in this moment and think of the rest as icing on the cake.

It's the cake that counts.

Break Time

No matter what your mind is telling you, realize it may or may not be true. If you're filled with loving thoughts of gratitude, groove on. If you're spending time worrying about what's going wrong in the world, give yourself a break. That is, unless you can do something about it.

Then hop to it.

Honesty Equals Intimacy

Real intimacy and friendship only happen when you're true to yourself. Trying to be what someone else wants you to be keeps things superficial. When you express yourself authentically, you attract people who are in alignment with the real you. Those who aren't just naturally fall away.

Let the real you shine.

Eliminate Should

When you 'should' on yourself or others, it only makes matters worse. If you want something to change, quickly acknowledge it as it is, turn your focus to what you want and then move on. You energize whatever you give your attention to.

Feed what you like.

Success

Take responsibility for the things you have control over, like your effort and your attitude. Let go of the stuff you can't control, like others' approval or being the best in the world. You can't fail unless you give up. If you lack success, it's by your own definition.

Redefine it.

The Alchemy of Difference

All relationships experience conflict now and then. Honest expression naturally gives rise to a diversity of opinion. When there is mutual respect and a desire to understand one another, what begins as conflict, can end in valuable growth. Like the sand in an oyster...

Friction makes the pearl.

Thought Programming

You came into life with certain capacities - that's your hardware. Your ability to operate optimally and avoid crashing is largely due to your programming - that's your software. Every thought you think is like creating code. Negative thinking is writing your own software virus. Even if it doesn't crash the hard drive, it saps energy, makes it sluggish and stresses the machine.

Code for Joy.

True Love

A little girl was suffering from a rare and serious disease. Her only chance of recovery appeared to be a blood transfusion from her 5 year-old brother, who had miraculously survived the same disease and developed the antibodies to combat the illness. The doctor explained the situation to her little brother and asked the little boy if he would be willing to give his blood to his sister.

He hesitated for only a moment, took a deep breath and said, "Yes, I'll do it if it will save her." As the transfusion progressed, he lay in bed next to his sister and smiled as he saw the color returning to her cheeks. Then his face grew pale and his smile faded. He looked up at the doctor and asked with a trembling voice, "Will I start to die right away?"

The real thing.

The Sweet Spot

Be confident, but not arrogant. Be quick, but not rash. Be dedicated, but not driven. Exercise control, but don't be a freak.

Seek balance.

You're the Captain

Sometimes things go your way, sometimes they don't. Control of external circumstances is often out of your hands. But one thing is for certain: you're always in charge of how you feel. You're the master of your own emotional ship and completely free to tack to any emotional course you choose.

Sail away.

Love 'em and Leave 'em

Unpleasant situations or people may simply be there to provide you with the opportunity to establish better boundaries. Be honest with yourself about how you really feel. Take kind and appropriate action in alignment with your truth.

If necessary, leave 'em with love.

Groove or Rut

Developing healthy daily practices brings about positive progress. Be careful not to confuse daily practice with unconscious repetition. One is a decision to cultivate mastery. The other is a habit, which may be masking stagnation. Pursue mastery and drop the routine.

Same action, different outcome.

Be Open

It takes curiosity to learn. The more you listen, the more you learn. Opening your mind to the ideas of others requires vulnerability. It also opens the door to a deeper and more genuine appreciation of the intelligence and wisdom around you.

Open mind, open heart.

Beliefs Define Reality

Your beliefs determine the way you see life. If you like what you see, your beliefs are in alignment with your desires. If you don't, look for the beliefs that aren't serving you.

Realign.

Resistance Is Futile

When your self-image doesn't match the feedback you receive from the world, try something new. Rather than resist and defend, welcome the message as a gift. When you accept the reality of the situation as it is, you're truly ready to change it.

Correct and continue.

Rise After Falling

Japanese proverb: Fall seven times. Get up eight. What matters most, falling or getting up? It depends on how many times you get up.

Rise and shine.

Love Yourself

The most profound thing you can do to improve your life is to love yourself more. Find the ways you judge yourself as less-than and then treat yourself the way you would treat a child just learning to walk. Encouragement enhances growth. Criticism retards it.

Cheer yourself on.

The Most Powerful You

Finding your authentic Self is a big part of what the journey of life is all about. That Self is the greatest gift you have to offer. When you love and accept yourself, you're free to *be* yourself.

Be you now.

Life Unfolds Perfectly

No matter how it may seem from your current perspective, life unfolds with perfection. All that came before led you to where you are now. Would you trade any of those difficult lessons? Most people wouldn't. Although they weren't always easy, look what you learned! Truth is, it was the resistance that made it seem so difficult.

Resist less, flow more.

Balance Pays Off

Whether high or low, emotional extremes wreak havoc. A calm, centered awareness allows you to view 'good' and 'bad' with equanimity. The right perspective carries you through the ups and downs of everyday life with stability and poise.

It's called chillin'.

Who Do You Think You Are?

The purpose of nearly every belief you have is to maintain your identity. Look at the issues you 'stand' for and examine how they support your idea of yourself. Next time you meet up with somebody who holds opposing beliefs, remember that they're just trying to maintain their identity too…

Just a different one.

What You Resist, Persists.

Do your beliefs make you feel good about yourself and your world? It may seem ironic, but finding what's right in every situation puts you in the optimal frame of mind for positive change. Accept what is and...

Make adjustments as necessary.

Adapt with Flexibility

Change is the only constant in the Universe. Resist it and you experience discomfort. Accept it and you align with flow. When you're in flow, you can help create the change you desire.

Go with the flow.

Everything Is Just Right Now

Take a look at something that irritates you. Entertain the possibility that this irritation is a gift containing information about *you*. The world you perceive is a reflection of how you see yourself. Try to drop the need for things to be different and look for the perfection in what is.

Including you.

Thoughts Give Birth

Everything begins with a thought. Whether consciously or not, desired or not, you give birth to your reality by the thoughts you think. Use protection and conceive on purpose. Gestate consciously and deliver through a labor of love.

Thought control begets desired offspring.

Acceptance Transforms

Have you ever considered that your interpretation of most things is an automatic response triggered by your ego to maintain your identity? Satisfaction or discomfort result when outer circumstances match or conflict with your self-image. When you argue with reality, you suffer. Make peace with what is and watch it change.

Take a load off.

Expect Love and Abundance

Never cease to dream because you fear disappointment. Success is more likely when you expect love and abundance. Your expectations condition your reality.

Expect the best.

Relax and Enjoy Life

Worry never helps. If your intention is for the highest purpose of all involved, then your best is always good enough. Since you can never know for sure what the highest purpose is, let go of attachment to the results and watch with curiosity as the beauty of life unfolds.

It always does.

No Need to Forgive

When you understand the truth, that life is happening *for* you, forgiveness becomes a moot point. If everything occurs in order to serve your evolution, nothing needs to be forgiven.

It all supports you.

Direct Your Attention Wisely

Energy flows where attention goes. If you want to fuel something into existence, focus on it. Just make sure it's something you actually want. Life doesn't make distinctions about whether it will benefit you or not. It leaves that up to you. It's your life and your choice.

Free will.

Your Conditioning Creates Your Reality

Two people can experience the same situation in drastically different ways. Each person projects their own filters, beliefs and values onto external phenomena. Right and wrong are not always clear-cut. Once you understand this, it's a lot harder to be self-righteous.

And easier to be accepting.

Listen Before the Message Gets Louder

When your body goes out of balance, it gives you signals. If you listen and take corrective measures, it usually shifts back into balance. If you don't, the signals get louder and stronger. All of life is like that. The messages can be found in whatever is before you. If you like what you see, be grateful. If not, take corrective measures.

Don't make life scream at you.

Feelings Tell You About You

The way you see life tells you most about your own beliefs. If something makes you feel uncomfortable, you have a belief that is 'arguing' with reality. Changing the outside to make you feel better is a never-ending battle. Questioning beliefs that aren't in alignment with 'what is' brings peace of mind.

And makes you happy.

Are You Balanced?

At the end of your life, which door would you like to walk through? 1) Worked enough; 2) Played enough; 3) Loved enough; 4) Served enough; or 5) All of the above? Most people would probably pick door number 5. And most people probably need to do some catching up on door number 2. How about you?

Get to playing!

Guilt Is Misguided

Guilt and shame seem to serve the practical purpose of helping you learn from your mistakes. However, this is based on the faulty thinking that you could have done other than you did. If it were possible for things to have happened differently, they would have. What appear to be mistakes are valuable tools to help you learn, not reasons to punish yourself.

Learn the lesson and move on.

Love Starts with You

You can only love others to the extent that you love yourself. Don't be concerned with the idea that loving yourself is selfish. It's not. Appreciate, accept, forgive and be kind to yourself. See how good that feels?

Share the love.

Open to the Bounty

Have you ever noticed feeling less than thrilled when good fortune comes to someone else? It only happens when you aren't allowing that same abundance to come to you. There's only one person stopping you from having what you want.

You.

A Happy You Makes a Happy Two

Want a happy relationship? Make yourself happy first. Then see what you can do to make your partner happy. Happiness comes from within. Waiting for your mate (or anybody else) to make you happy will only result in a long, unsatisfying delay. You're in control of your happiness.

Good news!

Pick Your Battles

When you disagree with someone, rather than immediately expressing your contrary opinion, listen carefully to what they're saying. Let them know when you understand where they're coming from. Unless it's really important, save the energy-depleting disagreement for something that matters. You probably won't change their mind anyway.

It's disarming.

Fear Dumbs You Down

Fear is an instinctual response to a perceived threat. It shifts your thought processes to the more primitive part of your brain causing you to react with less finesse and intelligence. It prevents you from playing a bigger game. Next time you make a decision out of fear...

Think again.

Instant Mood Change

If you find yourself in a sour mood or notice something tugging at you slightly below the surface, try this easy technique for relief. Stop what you're doing for a moment, pay attention to your body and just notice how it feels. When you face a feeling head on and give it the attention it's wanting, it often just slinks away.

Feelings need to be felt.

Empathy the Easy Way

It's easy to feel compassion and empathy for people you identify with, but what about the rest? When you realize the truth, that your judgments are really more about you than they are about them, you lighten up. Increased self-awareness takes the place of judgment and compassion begins to flow.

Naturally.

Enjoy Life Now

Notice the aspects of your life that are going well and take a moment to appreciate them. While goals and dreams are great to pursue, don't believe for a second that the things you want in the future mean you can't enjoy the marvelous perfection of your life this very instant.

Revel.

First You, Then Everything Else

The way to change anything in your life is to change yourself first. You may succeed in fixing the outside world in small ways, but it'll only be temporary. There's only one way to experience real change.

Inside out.

The Truth about Us All

We should all walk around with a sign posted on our foreheads that reads: "Please don't take anything I say or do personally. I'm as self-oriented as you are. Everything I say and do is consciously or unconsciously aimed at pleasing me, even when it seems like I'm trying to please you."

Refreshing.

Open to Possibility

Life has a way of fulfilling your expectations. When you look for the good and expect the best, that's usually what you'll find. The more you find it, the more you expect it.

Magic feedback loop.

Pick Your Battles

Everything you encounter in life is *for* you! Your interpretation and response create your experience moment by moment. Whether you accept, resist, love or fear what is, life is going to do its thing. In the meantime, you get to be with your experience.

Dig it.

The One You Need to Forgive

Nothing anyone ever does is about you. When you get this, the idea of forgiveness is a moot point. If someone offends you, take a moment to question if you're really just angry with yourself for being in the situation in the first place.

Then let yourself off the hook.

Your Mood, Your Call

Learning to be content right here and now is the best skill you can develop. You perfect it by looking for what's right. Avoid the downward spirals of worry, fear and pity. It's good to acknowledge your feelings, but don't spend time stewing. Whatever you focus on brings that frequency into your vibration.

Focus wisely.

Telegraph Your Life

To create your dreams, look in the direction you want to go and feel the joyful emotion of fulfillment. Act as if they've already come true. Then do it again.

Here they come.

Who's Driving Your Life?

Your experience of life is determined by how you view and interpret events. When you're conscious of your thought patterns, you create your experiences on purpose. When you're not, your feelings are based on conditioning you didn't even choose. Awareness puts you in the driver's seat.

Drive Consciously.

Better Bumper Stickers

You've probably seen the bumper sticker, "If you aren't outraged, you aren't paying attention." Here's a new one: "If you aren't grateful, you aren't paying attention." Either could be true for you - it just depends on where you put your focus. Your experience of life is created by the thoughts you cultivate. Which do you prefer to be...

Outraged or grateful?

Love Matters Most

At the end of life, no one ever wishes that they had spent more time working. What really matters is how kind you were and how much love you spread. It's never too late to start.

Love fest.

Want What You Have

When you focus on gratitude for all you have now, your energetic vibration is tuned to abundance. When you focus on what you want, but don't yet have, you're attention is on lack. It matters which you choose because what you focus on expands.

Grow gratitude.

Turn It Over

There is an intelligence within you that beats your heart, digests your food, grows your hair and does a gazillion other things that you don't ever have to think about. The same intelligence will take care of all your troubles too, if you just let it. All you have to do is ASK and then get out of the way. Well, you'll still have to handle a few little things like, booking your flights, depositing your checks...

And choosing which shoes to buy.

Split Second Decision

You have a choice about the way you respond to every situation. Next time you find yourself feeling aggravated, pause before you react and just observe what's happening inside you. Ask yourself how it's *for* you. Maybe it's to help you develop patience or learn to set boundaries. Once you see the gift, you'll be in the right space to respond appropriately.

Open to it.

As Within, So Without

It's a natural law of the Universe. The more you give, the more you receive. If you want more love, give more love. If you want more money, spread some around. If you want to be heard, listen. If you want more friends, be one.

Simple.

Nurture Your Enthusiasm

When you embody enthusiastic anticipation for something, it creates a positive, receptive energy that opens your mind and heart to possibility. When you're open, you're dynamic, energized, upbeat and ready for inspiration and success.

No known down side.

Highest Purpose for All Involved

When you always want the highest purpose for all involved, you understand a deep truth: you will only allow for yourself what you want for others. When grace shines on anyone, seize the opportunity…

And be happy.

Respond

When you have enough conscious awareness to respond to life rather than react to it, you become the creator of your own experience. There's always a split second between what happens and what you do about it. Being able to step into that split second and choose consciously makes all the difference in the world.

R.S.V.P.

Manage Your Energy

Focusing on what you like generates energy. Focusing on what you don't like depletes it. Make a practice of noticing where your attention goes and how it feels. Is your thinking building you up or dragging you down? You're in charge.

Charge up.

Time Is Relative

If you don't pay attention to time in music, no one can play with you. If you ignore time in your commitments, no one will *want* to play with you. When it comes to time in healing, whether physically or emotionally, you can't rush it. When you have a deadline, you can't slow it down. While time is having its way with you, there's only one remedy.

The present moment.

Internal Architecture

Your thoughts and words create the blueprint for your life's design. When you're aware of this, you can make choices that are in alignment with what you want. When you're not, your unconscious conditioning builds your life its way.

Build castles with awareness.

Enjoy Yourself

When you truly enjoy yourself, you're a joy to be around. Looking for someone else to fulfill you is not a winning strategy. Their job is to enjoy their life their way, just as your job is to enjoy yours your way. When you're both already fulfilled, there's no expectation and no burden.

Just joy, enjoying jointly.

Loosen the Knot

Think of something in your life that you have no control over and you're unhappy about. Now, let go and accept it. Relax and allow it to be. Tying your self up in knots doesn't help. Remember, all things come to pass.

Untangle.

Life Is What You Believe It Is

If you believe life is hard, it is. If you believe life is good, it is. If you believe life is miraculous...it *is*!

What do you believe?

Practice New Patterns

Creating a big story about what you don't like, only makes things worse. It's good to be aware of your preferences, but don't focus your attention on the negative. Knowing what you don't like helps you know what you do.

Energize *that*.

Create with Intention

Clarify your intentions and your life will move toward them. Like a flower bends toward the sun for its precious energy, your experience of life follows your attention. Be clear about the quality and direction of your focus.

And bloom.

You're a Masterpiece

With the right attitude, each experience you have can be *for* you. Even situations that push your buttons show you where you're attached to things going exactly your way. When you relax and accept what is, as it is, you begin to see how everything is perfect. Like a painting that benefits from each preceding brushstroke...

Life's a masterpiece in the making.

Weed Your Thoughts

Most things in life respond to your loving attention. Just like a garden when you weed it. If there's something that's bugging you, try weeding out your negative thoughts about it. Then, give it the healing power of your love. If it still doesn't respond...

Weed *it* out.

Tuning Your Vibration

The feelings you focus on create your energetic vibration. That's a good thing if they're happy ones. If they're negative, critical or angry, you're tuning your dial to a station with a lot of static. Focus on love and gratitude for clarity.

Vibrate happily.

Free Will

While you don't have control over everything in your life, you do over the one thing that matters most...

Your attitude.

Discernment Not Judgment

It's your birthright to live life your way. When others do things you don't like, take note without making them wrong. If it really bugs you, take *action* without making them wrong. Wrong to you may be right to them.

And vice versa.

What's Driving You?

When fear runs your life, you play small. When love is your driver, the sky's the limit. It's a choice you make every moment. Which do you choose?

Love or fear?

Truth Is Relative

No matter how real your experience seems to you, it's not always an accurate indicator of the truth. Experience is just perception filtered through conditioning. Different filters create different experiences. Good to remember when your perception doesn't feel good.

Filter change.

It's Not Personal

If someone says something that hurts your feelings or angers you, it isn't personal. Their conditioning is simply colliding with yours. When you meet it without resistance or defensiveness, it's deflected and no harm is done. If you match it, it's like a head on collision.

Swerve.

Deliberate Mastery

You'll eventually master whatever you practice on a daily basis. It doesn't matter if it's an artistic talent, conscious awareness or a bad attitude; consistency will make you a pro. Look into your habits to see if you're practicing things you actually want to get good at.

Master with intention.

Wake Up

If you've forgotten about the ocean of abundance flowing around you, open your eyes and take a look. Abundance is not something you acquire. It's something you tune into. Tune in and turn on the tap.

Let it flow.

The Journey Is the Destination

Your life moves through time as a car moves through space. Naturally you'd like it to go where you want. Just don't forget that in life, like on road trips, the journey is often the best part.

Life is a trip.

Make Lemonade

When you have expectations that aren't met, you can either make the best of it, or nurture your disappointment. When you look for the positive in a situation, you won't be disappointed. When you go with disappointment, you will be.

Your choice.

Immediate Relief

Every problem is exactly what you think it is because it's just a perception in your mind. When you shift your attention from the problem and ask your Inner Presence to bring you into right thinking, you gain a different perspective. Relief is on the way.

Just ask.

Gift in Every Moment

Everything you see in life exists to serve you in some way. If it's not immediately apparent, look again.

It's your present.

Feeling Good

When you acknowledge the aspects of your life that are going well, you put yourself in the most conducive frame of mind to expand that list. Feeling good about yourself enhances every part of your life.

Beats the alternative.

Ruled by Thought

Some thoughts can stress you out and make you sick. Others can heal you. Love and gratitude lift you up. Judgment and anger give you a hangover. Seems like what you think about shapes your experience of life.

Bingo.

Silent Communication

If you're having difficulty communicating effectively with someone, imagine talking to that person's Inner Presence. Tell them what you have to say and then envision the two of you standing together under a spotlight of mutual understanding.

Expect magic.

This Moment Gives Birth to the Next

When you accept what's happening in this moment, the next one will take care of itself. You set yourself up for the way you experience the next moment by the way in which you meet the one you're in.

Meet it with love.

Unfettered Access

When you're focused on an issue without worry, your natural brilliance is freely accessible. Concerning yourself with negative outcomes distracts you and shuts you down.

Keep your eyes on the prize.

Effortless Flow

Life flows effortlessly when you relax and drop your strategies. Recognize what you want, let go of attachment to results, focus on fulfillment, listen for guidance within and take action as necessary. You'll *marvel* at how life itself works out all the details for you.

Allow it.

Tell the Truth

Every time you don't tell your truth, you set yourself apart from your authentic Self and go a little out of balance. If your life feels chaotic and confusing, look where you aren't being completely honest about how you really feel. Telling the truth naturally aligns you with the people, places and conditions that float your boat.

Happy Sailing.

Life Is What You Think It Is

Everyone's perception of reality is filtered through the lens of their unique conditioning. That makes as many interpretations as there are people. Relatively speaking, everyone's right. Absolutely speaking, nobody is. The Truth is 'what is' before any judgment, qualification or spin. Perception is not Truth, but what you see is real...

For you.

Energy Flows Where Attention Goes

There's an infinite variety of things to focus on. Looking for the good sets you up to actually find them. Finding them feels good.

Virtuous cycle.

Word Up

When you finally stop talking about things that make you unhappy, you stop being unhappy. Feeding yourself dissatisfaction can never result in making you feel satisfied. Words have creative force. Verbalize what you want.

Think twice, speak once.

The School of Life

If you interpret every experience as an opportunity to learn something about yourself, you will never see anything as all bad. You'll look for the lesson and try to understand your role in creating the situation. This is the way to look life straight in the eyes.

Honestly.

Master the Moment

Paying too much attention to problems and people you don't like downgrades your vibration. Criticism and judgment pollute your now. Opinions are fine...

Just don't stew.

Adjust and Adapt

When life disappoints you, realize it's only because your expectations are out of alignment with reality. Just as you can't change the weather, reality simply is what it is. There's not much more you can do than correct and continue on.

Happily or grumpily.

Love and Approval

Everyone is looking for love and approval. Behavior that disregards or offends is unconscious and not personal. You don't have to like everyone you meet, but it's easy to be forgiving when you remember that *everybody* is doing the best they can. If they could do it better, they would.

That includes you.

You Are Worthy

Most people suffer from a sense of unworthiness that they developed in early childhood. Even though it's not true, it can be difficult to convince yourself otherwise. Next time you notice it creeping up on you, face it, feel it and see it for what it is: an inaccurate perception created unintentionally by you and your caretakers. Shine the light of your awareness on the feeling.

It only lives in the dark.

Control Yourself

Rather than trying to control your friends, family or mate, work on controlling yourself. When you change the inside, the outside automatically changes.

Looking glass.

A Brand New Day

You know the expression 'if you forget history, it's bound to repeat itself'? Consider this: When you focus on the past, you *are* repeating it. Understanding the power and richness of this moment makes you think twice about wasting it on the past.

All you need is *now*.

Unique, Not Special

Any need to see your self as special comes from a wound of inadequacy. If you weren't feeling insufficient in some way, you wouldn't need to see others as being less than you. If you think you're special, realize it's a gift showing you a wound.

Feel it to heal it.

Authentic Achievement

Authentic achievement can bring great joy and satisfaction. However, when accomplishment is compulsively driven by the fear of not being good enough, your driver will take you on a wild goose chase. You know it's authentic when you're doing it for the love of it.

No fear involved.

Happiness First

Don't pin your happiness on some arbitrary standard... "I'll feel good when..." Feeling good is a choice you make each moment. Jump into feeling good now. Then go after your goals.

Feel it first.

Worry Is a Waste

Worry only makes you less effective at dealing with what's bothering you. Focusing on fearful thoughts energizes them. Take the peaceful approach: feel your feelings, ask your Inner Presence for guidance, decide to do the best you can and then visualize success. The suffering caused by worry is often worse than what you fear.

Unnecessary.

Practice Letting Go

Knowing something intellectually is different from embodying it. You can know that worrying causes stress and stress causes illness, but until you put that knowledge into practice in your daily life, it's just a concept.

No worries mate.

What Defines Your Life?

Do you see problems or challenges, constraints or opportunities? Are you demoralized or inspired to innovate? Is that person annoying or are they teaching you something about yourself? There's no right answer to these questions, but one thing is for sure...you can view life anyway you want.

Your call.

Your Choices Matter

The thoughts you think and the actions you take not only create your experience of life in this moment, they determine the quality of your future. Consciously cultivate balance and joy *now*.

The future will follow suit.

Avoid Cheap Thrills

When you find yourself harshly judging someone, quickly ask your Inner Presence to transform the thought into one of tolerance and understanding. Judgments make you temporarily feel superior, but before you know what hit you, the judgment boomerangs right back at you.

Don't get whacked.

Don't Wait

The majority of life is composed of making plans and taking care of business. Very few moments are spent basking in the glory of accomplishment. Don't wait for outside acknowledgement.

Be a winner right now.

Identify with What's Real

Are you identified with your possessions, position, looks or talents? There's an easy way to tell if you are. Just imagine yourself without them. How does it feel? All these things can be taken away. Develop that which can't be.

Internal wealth.

No Other Way

It's erroneous to think you could have done something differently than you did. Every circumstance in your life led to that behavior. While you might see how you would choose differently in the future, don't waste a moment in regret. Now that you know better, be grateful for the lesson.

Bygones.

What's Your Story?

You live in whatever story you tell yourself. No matter what aspect of your life you're focused on, *your* story is only one of many possible interpretations. Does it empower you, upset you, delight you or frighten you? It's your choice.

Every moment.

Circulate It

Both the Sea of Galilee and the Dead Sea receive the same water from the River Jordan. The Galilee gives by allowing the water to flow through it. The Dead Sea holds it. Life is teaming and abundant all along the Galilee. The still water of the Dead Sea evaporates and leaves a toxic environment that supports nothing. Whether with water, money or love...

Let it flow.

Commit to Happiness

While making your to-do list, bucket list, life-goals list or vision-board, add this to it: "Become a master at feeling joyful." After all, that's what you think all those other things on your lists will do for you. You could just cut to the chase.

Shortcut.

Let Go

Holding on to hurt...hurts you! When you experience a hurtful situation, acknowledge it, feel it, forgive it and then let it go. The event only happened once. How many times will you hurt yourself by reliving it over and over?

Once is more than enough.

Intention and Commitment

If you want something, formulate a clear intention and then commit to it with all your heart. That commitment will guide every decision and action.

Commitment is key.

One Exception

Everything that happens in life is for your benefit. Except for when you think it's not. Look for *that* habit and...

Kick it.

Please Yourself

You can please some of the people all of the time, and all of the people some of the time...wait a minute, that's all too difficult. Since the outside world is just a mirror of your inside, work on pleasing yourself. Then everyone else will seem pleased.

The direct path.

Conscious Authenticity

Do you try to control situations, seek approval from others or say yes when you really feel like saying no? These are strategies to cover up feeling out of control, inadequate or a fear of being disliked. Next time you catch yourself wanting to act this way, try feeling the underlying feelings instead.

Feel them to heal them.

It's Sensational

Physical pain is just a sensation until the mind gets involved and makes a full report. It's the same with emotional pain. The story about it is what makes it hurt. While it's difficult to stop the onslaught of the narrative, it *is* possible. Next time you catch your mind making things worse by sensationalizing...

Stop it.

Be Here Now

Everything you need is available right now. If that's not your experience, you may not be focused on the here and now. Turn your awareness to what's happening where you are, in this very moment and see for yourself.

It's true.

Double Standard

When other peoples' behavior bothers you, it's usually because you view it as unloving. When you judge them, rather than see them with compassion, your behavior matches theirs. Jump off that wavelength.

Change begins with you.

Intellect and Intuition

A strong intellect is a handy tool. It's great to be able to retain facts and weave them together cleverly, win arguments and explain things. But your heart and intuition are where you'll find your truth. Besides, your intellect doesn't love...

Your heart does.

Edit the Script

If others aren't fitting so well into the boxes you've created for them, realize it's not personal. Their job is to live life *their* way, not yours. Just because they're not saying their lines according to your script, it doesn't mean you can't still love them.

Rewrite their part.

Reality Rules

You create your experience of life by the way you see it. If you don't love it, you may be resisting something. When you make friends with reality, life unfolds with flow. Even the parts that don't seem so great now will soon reveal their purpose.

Accept and flow.

Grist Is Grace

Problems teach you where you need to change the focus of your attention. It's usually away from difficulties and on to solutions. Focus on what you'd like to see, not on what you don't like. Your attention is fuel.

Feed the right fire.

Underlying Truth

When making decisions, always do what *feels* right. Making choices based on what you *think* will make others happy is confusing because you can never know what they really want. When you follow your heart, life flows harmoniously. What's good for you is often good for all.

Genius.

Position Versus Preference

If you're so sure of your position that you can't budge, you're bound to experience conflict. People have such varied life experiences that what's true for you is often not equally true for them. When you remember this, you soften your stance. What's next is inevitable...

More happy moments.

Thoughts Are Things

Notice the next thought that comes into your mind. Check to see if it's loving, judgmental or neutral. It's powerful to be aware of the quality of your thoughts. Thoughts create feelings that create moods that create perceptions that create experiences...

That make up your life.

The Power of Embodiment

When you're nervous, you have butterflies in your stomach. When you're anxious or fearful, your blood pressure rises. When you're stressed out, your immune system is taxed. When you're grateful, you're relaxed and at ease. All these conditions start with your thinking. That's really good news because you're in charge of that.

Right?

Happy Journey = Happy Destination

Your life is a journey. How happy you are is determined by how well you travel through life. If you postpone the pleasures along the way, thinking that the reward is the *destination*, you're in for an unpleasant surprise. Unhappy trips don't result in happy arrivals.

Happy trips do.

Sparkle

Every so often you meet a person with an appealing twinkle in their eyes. They seem to emit a radiant ray of positive energy that just feels good to be around. It's the unconditional acceptance and appreciation of what is that makes them beam.

Get *your* sparkle on.

Happiness Is a Choice

It's easy to find things that don't quite meet your requirements. But you've only really mastered the *art* of life when you're able to find something to appreciate even in the most trying of situations.

You've got to look to find it.

Life Is Full of Presents

You are loved. Everything you see exists for you. Even when it seems that something's missing, remember that nothing ever really is. Whether it's a blessing or a lesson, there's a gift in every present...

Moment, that is.

Adjust and Continue

If you think of every experience as an opportunity to learn, you'll never fail. Just like the robotic vacuum cleaner, every time something blocks your path, just back up, alter your course and continue on your way. The obstructed route just informs you where not to go.

Can't fail.

Addicted to Drama

Talking about your troubles rarely makes you feel better. Next time you find yourself 'sharing' your feelings, check your motivation. Make sure you're not in either judgment or victim mode. Give yourself the attention you're looking for by actually feeling your feelings.

Then drop the story.

Attention Creates Your Life

If you put your attention on what might go wrong, you'll most certainly come up with plenty of possibilities. There's no end to the problems and predicaments your mind can create when you let it. The same is true when you turn your mind toward opportunities and solutions.

The sky's the limit.

Make the World a Better Place

Some think the fate of humanity can only be improved by force. Others are convinced it'll happen by converting everyone else to their point of view, political system or religious persuasion. But real progress will only be made when the collective consciousness grows. When you evolve your own consciousness, you improve the world. Take the truly effective path and...

Change yourself first.

About the Authors

Jarl Forsman

Jarl Forsman lives on a houseboat in Sausalito, California with her husband and co-author, Steve Sekhon. A forty year practice of Tai Chi and other forms of meditation, psychotherapy, hypnotherapy, spiritual counseling, dream work, daily journal writing, personal inquiry along with help from many teachers have informed her path of self-discovery. Jarl teaches Tai Chi and Qigong and maintains a diverse counseling clientele. She co-founded Gratitude Twenty Four Seven with Steve, to help herself and others raise their consciousness in order to enhance their fulfillment in life.

Steve Sekhon

Steve Sekhon draws from his earlier incarnation as an international urban planner when he worked in Cambodia, Bosnia-Herzegovina and Southern Sudan, all countries ravaged by civil war. These experiences helped him to realize that each person is fundamentally free to make choices regarding his own perception and interpretation of events. The way in which this is done has a profound impact on one's life. After nearly thirty years of studying Western mysticism, Eastern spirituality, diverse meditation techniques and fourteen years of daily Tai Chi practice, Steve and Jarl, started Gratitude Twenty Four Seven, a website designed to help others increase their self-awareness to live happier and more fulfilled lives.

Our intention is to help you grow happiness, harmony and love by overcoming limiting and erroneous beliefs that prevent you from expressing your full potential.

For a free subscription to Daily Insights or to sign up for online courses, please visit our website:

www.gratitudetwentyfourseven.com

For private coaching sessions or to contact Jarl and Steve, send an email to:

info@gratitudetwentyfourseven.com

www.ingramcontent.com/pod-product-compliance
Lightning Source LLC
Chambersburg PA
CBHW060151050426
42446CB00013B/2763